I0201710

DRIVERS

THE DEMISE OF A PROUD PROFESSION

SAMMY LEE GOTT

SH

Silkhaven Publishing, LLC

ISBN: 978-1-948997-45-4 (mobi)

ISBN: 978-1-948997-44-7 (epub)

ISBN: 978-1-948997-43-0 (paperback)

Library of Congress: 2020908045

Copyright (c) 2020, Sammy Lee Gott

(V1) – April 27, 2020

All rights reserved. No part of this book may be used or reproduced in any manner without the written permission of the author Sammy Lee Gott and the publisher Silkhaven Publishing, LLC with the exception in the case of brief quotations embodied in critical articles and reviews.

Printed in the United States of America.

Silkhaven Publishing, LLC does not have any control over and does not assume any responsibility for author or third–party Web sites or their content.

The scanning, uploading, and distribution of this book via the internet or via any other means without the permission of Silkhaven Publishing, LLC or Sammy Lee Gott is illegal and punishable by law. To obtain a copy of this novel, please purchase only through authorized electronic or print editions, and do not participate in or encourage electronic piracy of copyrighted materials.

❀ Created with Vellum

CONTENTS

ACKNOWLEDGMENTS

I want to thank my wife Jan for all the help and inspiration she gives me with my writing and life in general.

During the six years that I was a commercial driver I met so many wonderful drivers. They cared about the well-being and safety of their passengers and went out of their way to make sure the ride they were giving was an enjoyable experience.

INTRODUCTION

This book is about a profession that is slowly but surely disappearing. This is one driver's point of view of what is causing the demise of this proud profession—a driver who worked for numerous *Black Car* companies for six years and watched passengers being driven to their destinations in unsafe automobiles by drivers who were way underpaid and overworked.

This is a very old profession that started when the USA was very young. At that time drivers drove carriages and wagons behind horses. This was an age when your word meant something and good honest work gave you a chance to grow economically.

Then the day of the *Corporation* came and a dime product is sold for five dollars and the employee gets very little to produce the product or service, while the executives and stockholders get very rich.

"Show me an ultra-rich person, and I will show you a person, in a lot of cases, who has either underpaid their employees or overcharged their customers or both."
Sam Gott

In 2018 Lyft drivers on average earned about $30.00 per hour before paying all their expenses, while the CEO of Lyft made $41 million with stock options in 2017. Lyft was started in 2014 in 24 US Cities. **In 2018 Lyft was worth 15.1 billion dollars.**

The average Uber driver earns $8.80 to $11.00 per hour of driving after expenses. In 2018 Uber paid its top five executives a total of $6.8 million in salaries and cash bonuses plus $130 million worth of non-cash awards. Uber was started in 2009. **In 2018 Uber's net worth was 60 billion dollars.**

The average Greyhound hourly pay ranges from approximately $8.72 per hour for an Agent to $26.26 per hour for Diesel Mechanic. The average executive compensation was $231,539 a year with the highest compensated executive being paid $450,000. **In 2018 Greyhound had a gross income of $4.688 billion.**

Swift Transportation, one of the largest trucking companies in the United States, pays their drivers between $15.00 and $25.00 per hour. When factoring in bonuses and additional compensation, a Truck Driver can expect to make an average annual salary of $38,064. The median estimated compensation for executives at Swift Transportation Corporation including base salary and bonus is $234,400, or $112 per hour. The most compensat-

ed executive makes $700,000 annually. **In 2018 Swift Trans-portation was worth 3.51 billion dollars.**

Having worked with a Texas Chauffeurs License for almost six years in the Austin, Texas area, I earned $7.25 to $15.00 an hour plus tips (when the company I worked for did not steal them).

We will dig deeper into the mass thievery by transportation companies of their employees' moneys and talents in order to make the executives and stockholders rich. We will also talk about the over-regulations and fees from government entities. This is not happening only in transportation; it is happening all over the world in all industries.

1

WHY WRITE THIS BOOK?

I retired and decided to downsize. At that time I lived in San Antonio, Texas where I was raised and lived most of my life. I had spent forty-two years in the world of financial services. I have a Master's Degree in Financial Services and I was a practicing Certified Financial Planner (CFP) and a Registered Investment Advisor.

San Antonio had grown since I was a boy from 250,000 to 1,500,000. It seems that everybody in the world had found Texas and decided to move here. We took two years looking for a small Texas town to move to. All the big Texas cities have been taken over by the world. One could only see the Texas that I grew up in the small towns. We decided on Georgetown, Texas, a beautiful little town about forty miles north of Austin, Texas. A part of this town was a place called Sun City, Texas, a community built especially for people of age fifty-five and over.

Sun City in Georgetown, Texas is a community that has three golf courses, four workout gyms, six swimming pools, tennis courts, horseshoes, softball, shuffleboard, Bocce courts, 3 libraries, billiards and many other amenities; also many clubs for doing almost anything one might have a mind to do. In other words, if you get bored in Sun City it is your fault. I immediately started playing golf and horse-shoes. I even became the president of the horseshoe club.

One morning I got up and looked in the mirror and I said to myself "you can't do this for the rest of your life." I have always been an active person and I was not ready to be put out to pasture. I needed to do something to keep busy and my mind active while I continue to write my books. I took a little time that morning to sit down and think about what I wanted to do when I grew up. I knew that I did not want to get back into finance and investments. Forty-two years was enough of holding clients' hands and leading them through the maze of financial planning and investments all the while putting up with state and federal over-regulation of the industry. I found that 30% of my day was spent keeping up with the paper work that government entities required under their compliance regulations. This new phase of my life was not about making money. I had always made six figures plus most of my life. This new job had to be about what I would enjoy doing. Something not too hard but would be fun. I like people, I like cars and I like to drive.

I have always had this great regard for chauffeurs ever since I was a kid. I decided I would look into it and see what it would take to become a chauffeur. **The great adventure began.**

In the upcoming chapters I will talk about many different driving professions that in my opinion have been ruined by greedy employers and governments who over-regulate their businesses. I will get most of my talking points from my experiences working for six different charter and limousine companies and being around hundreds of drivers over a six-year period. Government entities do not look out for the safety of the drivers nor the public. They are very busy raking in fees and very lax in doing their jobs. As I said before, I was not doing this for the money, and it is a good thing I wasn't, because between the employers and the government, the average driver cannot feed his or her family. I do not believe I will get famous or rich from writing this book but I believe someone had to speak up for all the people who or trying to make a living or supplement their incomes by driving in the United States working long hours, going without sleep, putting up with management who does not know what they are doing and government entities who will let the transportation companies abuse their drivers at the expense of the customers' safety.

2

WHAT ARE WORKERS LOOKING FOR?

I am going to start this chapter with a little of my background so that one can see that I have been involved in the work force for over sixty years. I started at age 15 working at Drive-in Movies doing odd jobs. I bought my school clothes and supplies with the money I earned. I then enlisted in the military and spent eight long years protecting my country and our freedoms all for very low pay. I finally, with promotions, got up to $270.00 per month. During those eight years I worked part time at odd jobs in order to have enough money to take care of my family.

After getting out of the military I had a very large paper route that fed my family while I went to college on the GI Bill. I worked as assistant manager in a national auto paint business progressing to regional supervisor. I then went into the Insurance Industry where I spent twenty years working my way up to senior vice president in a fortune five hundred company. I have built companies to become profitable entities and I have been a self-employed consultant for many years. Please see the following resume:

CURRICULUM VITAE OF SAMMY LEE GOTT

www.sammyleegott.com

Experience: Counseling individuals and small businesses in financial, retirement, tax and estate planning. Building and servicing comprehensive financial programs including investments and risk management vehicles. Consulting, installing and servicing group insurance programs (Life insurance, AD&D, Health Insurance, Disability Insurance, Employee/member paid group programs)

EDUCATION:

- Master of Science in Financial Services (MSFS)

Professional Designations:

- Chartered Financial Consultant (ChFC)
- Chartered Life Underwriter (CLU)
- Life Underwriter Training Council Fellow (LUTCF)
- Accredited Asset Management Specialist (AAMS)
- Investment Advisor Compliance Specialist (IACS)

Licensure:

- Life and Health Insurance General Lines Agent
- Property and Casualty Insurance

2015 – Present Retired - Author

CURRICULUM VITAE OF SAMMY LEE GOTT

2002 – 2015 Sam Gott, Certified Financial Planner
1989 – 1999

Financial planning for individuals and business

Implement risk management and investment vehicles, fee-based financial planning, retirement, and estate planning. Design, implement, and service employee benefit programs including qualified retirement plans, group health, life, AD&D, disability insurance and employee/member paid insurance programs. Financial services operations consultant to Credit Unions.

. . .

1999 – 2002 Harborstone Investment Services

Senior Vice President & General Manager.

Managed a needs-based financial planning and investment company for Harborstone Credit Union, the third largest credit union in the state of Washington, including:

- Broker/dealer investment services
- Registered investment advisor services
- Life/health insurance agency
- Property/casualty insurance agency
- Employee benefit and retirement plans

Responsible for: goal setting, sales, product selection, revenue, profitability, expenses, and supervision of sales and administration personnel.

Office of Supervisor Jurisdiction (OSJ) Supervisor

Experienced in Broker-Dealer branch office operations and NASD compliance management, including suitability review, approving trades, accepting new accounts, security, advertising, books and records requirements.

Investment Advisor Compliance Specialist

Responsible for all functional aspects of investment advisor operations, including development, writing and updating Forms ADV, compliance manuals, supervisory policies and procedures, annual registrations and renewals on the CRD/IARD systems.

1983 – 1989 Alexander & Alexander

Senior Vice President, Executive Planning Services.

Executive Planning Services Department (an independent profit center), El Paso, TX; San Antonio, TX; Shreveport, LA; Monroe, LA and New Orleans, LA. Managed financial planning, investments, employee benefit planning, and sales/service of insurance products. Sales, implementation, and service of group insurance products/employee paid programs.

1981 – 1983 USAA Life Insurance Company

Manager, Estate Planning & Qualified Plans Departments.

Streamlined advanced marketing and tax-qualified retirement plans department to focus on marketing efforts, which resulted in increased profits. Designed/developed material for sales and service of group life insurance program. Trained sales and service staff.

1970 – 1981 Prudential Insurance Company

Sales Representative and Sales Manager.

Sales and service of life, health and group insurance programs. Received Prudential's top sales agent awards.

Managed the Corpus Christi, Texas office for four years. Hired and trained sales force for 20% of Texas.

———————

I PUT my resume above so that the reader might see that I do have a background in the business world and that I might know what I am talking about.

In my old age I have come to this conclusion, which I repeat:

Show me and ultra-rich person and I will show you a person, in most cases, who has underpaid their employees or has over-charged their customers or both.

Sam Gott

4

THE DISENCHANTMENT

According to an article written by Steve Hilton for Fox News entitled "Why I believe we need a positive populist revolution"; adjusted for inflation, the average American worker over the last forty-four years had a pay cut of 2%. In 1972 the average weekly salary was $736.86, in 2016 the average weekly salary was $723.67.

During this same period of time what cost $100.00 in 1972 in 2016 cost $574.16. Inflation played havoc with the buying power of the average worker. The rich got richer and the average workers saw their incomes go down and/or their jobs go away.

Instead of corporations concentrating on shareholder value, corporations need to concentrate on employee value. Why do employees think that companies do not care about anything but boosting their profits? It's because they know that making shareholders more money is the number one priority of all corporations and not taking care of their employees.

The second priority of most corporations is making big bonuses for the executives. The extreme salaries and bonuses for executives are really an insult to the average employee. Common sense tells them that someone being paid millions of dollars is overpaid. The average Lyft driver earns $30.00 an hour before expenses while the CEO of Lyft earned $42 million in 2017 with stock options. Does anyone think that the Lyft drivers thought this was fair?

Corporations are going to have to do what Delta Airlines just did. Delta split $1.6 billion of 2019 profits with the employees. In other words Delta's profit sharing plan was really a profit sharing plan. Delta was picked as the number one airline in 2019. *If a company takes care of their employees, their employees will take care of the company.* I believe all corporations' profits should be split three ways: employees get 30%, stockholders get 20% and the company keeps the rest.

The average male cannot earn enough to feed and take care of his family. So the mother in the home has to work outside the home in order to help. Just think about this, in the last forty-four years have we seen the decline of our civilization because of children not being raised properly. When both parents have to work in order to provide for the family, good parenting suffers.

What is amazing is being underpaid is not the biggest reason for workers becoming disenchanted with their jobs. The biggest reasons are bad management and disrespect. In my opinion a lot of managers and executives of companies do not believe their employees are very bright. In an article written by Travis Bradberry, April 18, 2019, for News and Advice here are the major reasons employees leave companies:

1. They make stupid rules
2. They treat everyone equally
3. They tolerate poor performance
4. The don't recognize accomplishments
5. They don't care about people
6. They don't show people the big picture
7. They don't let people pursue their passions
8. They don't make things fun

AN ARTICLE IN *THE PLAYBOOK, Oct. 10, 2018* titled *"How to Get Your Employees Invested in Your Company"* had a great quote:

"When employees are not respected or valued as workers and human beings, when they are not served well and developed as people and professionals, when obstacles aren't cleared from their paths so they can perform well, when their voices aren't heard or are ignored, they experience disengagement, as early as weeks into a new job."

AT RANDSTAD US, researchers conducted a survey to nail down the top reasons people quit. Here are some of the findings:

- *More than half (59%) of the respondents felt their companies view profits or revenue as more important than how people are treated.*
- *Sixty percent of respondents had left jobs, or considered leaving, when they didn't like the direct supervisors.*
- *Fifty-three percent had left jobs, or considered leaving, because they believed their employers didn't recruit or retain high-performing individuals.*
- *Fifty-eight percent of workers said their companies didn't currently have enough growth opportunities for them to stay longer term.*
- *Sixty-nine percent said they would be more satisfied if their employers better utilized their skills and abilities.*
- *More than half (57%) said they needed to leave their current companies to take their careers to the next level.*

WELL, we have talked about bad managers; what does it take to be a good manager?

In a TalentSmart article titled "Things that make great bosses unforgettable," *Travis Bradberry gives us some insight:*

- *Great bosses are passionate, first and foremost*
- *They sacrifice themselves for their people*
- *Great bosses play chess not checkers*
- *They are who they are, all the time*
- *A great boss is a port in a storm*
- *Unforgettable bosses are human, and they aren't afraid to show it*

So now we have seen that the average worker is not only underpaid but over 50% of them are not managed properly. In future chapters we will see that in the driving industry the average driver is underpaid, mismanaged, and overworked. Also in too many driving jobs there are no workers benefits at all. In the six companies that I worked for (Charter Services and Limousine Services) not one of them provided or offered any of the following:

- Life Insurance
- Accidental/Dismemberment Insurance
- Health Insurance
- Disability Insurance
- Dental Insurance
- Vision Insurance
- Retirement Plan
- 401K Plan
- Workers Compensation*
- Clothing Allowance

I SPENT a number of years counseling, designing and implementing employee benefit programs for both small and large employers. We also counseled employees on their employee benefits so that they understood exactly what their employer was doing for them. If one wants to understand how much an employer cares for their employees just look at their benefits package.

The thinner the package the less the employer cares. Many times I would be talking to an employer and this statement would come out of their mouth: "It is very tough to find and keep good employees."

I would reply, *"If you take care of your employees, they will take care of you. You can't underpay them, overwork them and offer few benefits, and expect them to come to work for you or stick around. The good people will not apply or stay. What you end up with are the poor employees who can't find another job."*

THERE ARE a lot of workers in the transportation industry who work part time to supplement their primary job. Isn't it sad that people have to work two or three jobs to make enough money to take care of their families?

So what is the average worker looking for in a job?

Everyone wants to make enough money so they do not have to worry about too many expenses and too little income.

. . .

THEY WANT an atmosphere at the job that will have them wanting to come to work.

THEY NEED AND WANT RESPECT.

THEY NEED and want to know that their employer cares about them.

THEY NEED protections from all the risks that life throws at them.

NOW EMPLOYERS SAY, " That all costs money." Yes it does, but not near as much money as it takes to replace good employees that leave. When the employer retains good employees the company and all who work there make more money and the customers are well taken care of and satisfied.

There are two words that just do not go together —**quality** and **cheap.**

5

UBER

I am not going to say that UBER is the cause of the driving profession's demise, but they certainly are another nail in the coffin.

I thought at first that becoming an Uber driver was the perfect situation for me. Like so many others it looked so easy to get into and the income was going to be great. I am going to walk you through my thinking that convinced me that it was not for me.

HERE ARE the Uber Driver requirements:

- One must be at least 21 years old
- Licensed to drive in the US for at least one year, or three years if you're under age 23

- *Have access to a 4-door vehicle that is 10 years old or newer (in most cities). Many cities allow 15 years old or newer*
- *In-state auto insurance with your name on the policy*
- *In-state driver's license*
- *In-state license plates with current registration*
- *You must have a social security number*
- *Pass a background check and a driving record check*

It was sure easy enough to become an Uber driver but could you make any money at it? Let's look at some of the cost that a driver has to pay in the Austin, Texas area in order to drive for Uber:

Wear and tear on Vehicle – *I don't believe most people going to work for Uber realize that this a big cost. Let's say one owns a new car that is worth $35,000. If you work full time driving people it is easy to put on 75k to 100k of miles on your car each year. At that rate your car could be worn out in three years. Then what?*

Repairs on vehicle- *The more miles put on a vehicle the more that has to be repaired. The average mechanic's charge per hour for repairs is $125.00 and auto parts are very expensive. I have found with just family driving I spend $1,500+ in repairs to keep my vehicle running and I only put about 15,000 miles per year on it.*

New tires – *It has been my experience that I have to replace my tires about every 50,000 miles and the average cost of the tires I buy is about $125.00 per tire.*

Oil and fluid changes- *The recommended miles for oil changes* are three thousand miles and the average cost to change oil $35.00. That means that for every 100,000 miles driven one would change his or her oil 33 times, for a cost of $1155.00. Auto mechanics recommend that one should flush the transmission fluid, brake fluid and coolant every 100,000 miles. This costs at least $600.00

Cleaning of Vehicle- The more one uses one's vehicle, the more the vehicle has to be washed and vacuumed. Depending on your preference one can spend anywhere from $10.00 to $35.00 per wash.

Auto Insurance – Although Uber does carry insurance for their drivers the cost of a driver's personal insurance policy will go up in price.

Tolls – One cannot go anywhere in the Austin, Texas area without getting on a toll road. My average toll costs are about $50.00 per month just to do my personal errands. One can only imagine how high toll costs would be hauling people around Austin all day.

Gasoline – Let's estimate that the average price per gallon is $2.50 and my vehicle gets twenty miles to the gallon. This means that for every 100,000 miles I drive I will spend (100,000 divided by 20 multiplied by $2.50) $12,500 for gasoline.

Water and Miscellaneous for clients- The driver should be providing water, newspapers, and miscellaneous other things for the riders. This all has a cost to it.

Parking – If the driver has to wait any time at all for the rider or has to wait somewhere hoping to pick up a rider there are parking costs involved.

Eating out – If the driver has to pay for eating away from home this could be very expensive.

Traffic Tickets – *The more one drives the bigger the chances of getting tickets.*

Traffic Accidents – *The more one drives the bigger the chance for accidents and the additional cost of paying deductibles on your insurance.*

Clothing Costs – *Yes, you will have to dress better when driving, and that costs money.*

Payroll Taxes – *As an Uber driver I would have to pay all payroll taxes, which means that about 15% of every dollar of profit would go to Uncle Sam along with my income taxes.*

Uber says that a recent study shows their drivers nationwide earn an average of about $18.60 an hour before expenses. A report by the Economic Policy Institute found that Uber drivers pay averages only $9.21 after deductions for Uber fees.

I have just listed expenses that the driver has to pay. I was not impressed with the pay to me as a driver with all the liability I would be taking on. I was impressed how Uber managed to pass on almost all the expenses of driving people to the driver and managed to keep a big portion of the income pie. As I did my research I found out that Uber has about 833,000 drivers each year and the average driver lasts on the job for about three months. So I thought this was a high turnover ratio and that many drivers after driving three months have found that the return was not worth the hours worked. I decided that I would not work with Uber. It sounded good but when I put a pencil to it, two people out of the three involved in the ride did well and they were the rider and Uber. The driver, it seemed to be me, got the shaft.

Here are some statements from Uber drivers from an article in The Guardian by Michael Sainato published May 7, 2019

Vincent Suen: full-time Uber Driver for about two years in LA, "I wish I knew what I know now earlier, I was blindsided. If I knew about the expenses, how expensive it is to do this gig, I would not have gotten into it in the first place."

Ben Valdez: part-time Uber driver for nearly four years in LA, "the only way I can make a profit is through surge pricing during events for high demands. That's the only way I can make money, to drive during those peak times or I can't afford to drive for Uber."

Hrant Georgian: full-time driver in LA, "what I feel Uber does is like if you throw a seed to the birds and bring them to the cage and close the cage on them. Uber made it seem so good. I purchased a hybrid car, then they started little by little to reduce the wages."

Ali Razak: full-time Uber driver for five years in Philadelphia, "they are doing nothing for the drivers. All drivers are asking for is fair pay, and that's what Uber won't give to us. They are not willing to be transparent. They are willing to change the logo, they are willing to advertise, to spend millions on lobbying, but they are not willing to pay the drivers fairly."

Peter: full-time driver for one year in LA, "I pretty much have the lowest cost of living you can imagine in Los Angeles. I used to be able to afford that, recently Uber cut rate per mile by 25%. I have to work longer and longer hours in order to make rent. I want people to know how powerless you feel when your income comes from a faceless app and when you open it up one morning, things are just different and you're earning less money and there's no boss you can talk to, you weren't told about it, you just see your income is lower today and you just have to deal with it."

Uber's co-founder just sold Uber stock for $2.5B. I wonder how many of their drivers had to be on welfare to accomplish that?

6

THE GREAT ADVENTURE

One day into my retirement of eighteen months while playing horseshoes, a fellow player sat down beside me and asked me how my retirement was going. I replied that quite frankly I was getting tired of playing golf and horseshoes to fill my days. "Well Sam," he said, "I have an opportunity that you might want to consider." He began to tell me that he had started a business out of his home driving people back and forth to the airport, from Georgetown Texas to Austin, Texas. The airport is about a fifty-minute drive from Georgetown. The business was growing at such a rapid pace that he needed to find other drivers. I accepted and he outlined what I had to do to get licensed.

Well of course one had to already have a Texas Driver's License but there were other requirements: A notarized application, a Texas Department of Public Safety Report on your driving record plus a background check on your character before one could take the Chauffeur's licensing test. Of course all of these things had a fee attached, which the applicant had to pay.

The test was hilarious. One was supposed to be familiar with the Texas Driver's Handbook. I studied for many hours from this handbook in order to be prepared. When I tested I found that fifty percent of the questions came from MAPSCO Street Guide. The problem was the street guides that were in the testing area for our use were old with pages torn out of them. With pages gone it was difficult to answer some of the questions.

This was my first clue that the city of Austin, Texas was not paying attention to the transportation industry.

STILL EXCITED ABOUT BEING A CHAUFFEUR, I went to work at my first driving job. Let me say up front that I really enjoyed driving. The clients and I would have great conversations when the client wanted to talk. If they didn't want to talk then driving a good car in silence is fun. I met and interacted with great people. One day I would drive movie stars and the next day a high-ranking government official. I would say that ninety-five percent of the people I drove were very nice.

The charter service that I worked for drove people back and forth to the Austin airport. The driver could take IH 35 or the toll road. If the driver took IH 35, 80% of the time he did not know if he would get the client to his airplane on time. IH 35 runs from the Mexican border to the Canadian border. From the Mexican border to Dallas, Texas, on any day 250,000+ eighteen-wheelers would be on the road. One can imagine what this did to the traffic flow.

Now the toll road was a lot easier drive and ride for the client but it would cost $6.00 going and $6.00 coming back in tolls. The owner of the business did not want the driver to take toll roads because it cut into his profits. So he continuously raised hell about taking the toll road. Of course the rider wanted the driver to take the toll road because it was faster and a more comfortable ride. One cannot go anywhere in Austin, Texas without having to take a toll road—just another way for the government to steal your money.

Also if you are a commercial driver and you were going to the airport to pick someone up you would have to check in with the airport and they would charge you $3.50. Pay attention to the fees being charged to the company and the drivers by government entities in this book. One will find that they amount to a huge amount.

The pay for this driving gig was $7.25 per hour (minimum wage) plus tips except the tips were very light. I operated as an independent contractor. Most of our business came from a retirement community. I can attest that a lot of people over age 65 think that $10.00 is a big tip. The owner of the company told the clients, when he was the only driver, that they did not have to tip. It did not take me long to see that only 30% of the clients tipped. I talked to the owner about this because the $7.25 per hour was totally inadequate and without tips the drivers were underpaid. He said that he would start asking when the client called in if they wanted to add a tip. The tipping got better but not much. I made up a very professional sign that read "Gratuities Appreciated" and hung it on my mirror. In one month the riders tipping went from 30% to 85%. To my amazement this irritated the owner and he told me not to put the sign up because he was afraid it would scare off business. The owner was not concerned his drivers were not making enough money. I found out that when the people would call in and add a good tip to their bill the owner would take the run. The owner would also take the easy runs during the day and give his drivers the late night or early morning runs. On the late night runs the driver was instructed to watch the flight on a mobile application (late night flights usually late) and if the flight was late the driver would not get paid for the hours he waited for the flight to land. Sometimes this meant the driver would not get to bed before 4:00 AM.

I quit my first chauffeur job after only six months. That is how long it took me to realize that I was not being respected and I was being taken advantage of (yes, I am a little slow). With tips my hourly wage was about $10.00 an hour.

My second job was completely different. I worked for a company that all they had as vehicles were 29' limousines and 40' Hummer limousines. The runs were weddings, graduation parties, vineyard runs and executive parties. These runs were late night runs for the most part and the clients were very loud and very drunk. I was paid $15.00 an hour plus tips. With tips my pay was about $18.00 per hour. I was an independent contractor. The 29' limos were hard to drive because of their length but one got used to it. The vehicle was very smart looking but really uncomfortable for the riders.

The 40' Hummer Limos were almost impossible to drive. One could not make a right hand turn so mapping out your route making all left hand turns was imperative. Of course the Hummer was very popular with the younger generation and they loved to have their music blasting. I have a hearing disability from the military; I have lost about 15% of my hearing and their music was still too loud for me.

I believe that the best business to be in is the hearing aid business because this younger generation will be deaf by the time they are forty. I started turning off the back speakers and telling the kids that their music was so loud that a fuse blew and I would check it when we stopped. Because of the late nights and the drunks I had to contend with, that job lasted about six months. I have already told you I am a little slow.

My third job as a chauffeur was pretty nice actually. The company did have a 29' limousine but we seldom used it. The bulk of their business was hauling executives around Austin and other cities. I got to keep a stretch Lincoln at my home and drive it back and forth. The pay was $15.00 per hour plus tips (with tips about $18.00 per hour). I operated as an independent contractor. I like the owner and he was a fair person.

This owner ran two businesses. His second business was very profitable and his limousine business was barely profitable. He had older cars that needed a lot of repairs. Now days the cost of repairs on vehicles is out of sight and finding mechanics that are honest is getting harder all the time. This gig lasted about a year. One day the owner said he was shutting the limousine business down because it wasn't making enough money to make it worth his while.

My fourth driving job is where I received the bulk of my experience driving black cars. I worked for an international limousine franchise company for almost three years. This company considered the driver an employee.

They had been sued in the past because they were making the drivers clock in and out depending on the amount time the driver had to sit and wait for the client. In other words, if the driver took a rider to a location and had to wait for the rider to finish his business and then take him back to where he picked him up, the driver was told to clock out when he dropped the rider off and clock back in when the rider came back to the car. This could mean that the driver would sit and wait, sometimes hours, without getting paid.

The international company would book rides from people all over the world and send work to the local franchise. For about six months out of the year this would keep the drivers very busy. Each ride the company booked they would automatically add a 20% tip for the driver. These tips bumped our hourly pay to $20.00 to $23.00 dollars an hour. This was the only thing that was good about working for this company. I am going to list below some of the many bad things one encountered working for this company.

1. *A driver can only work 12 consecutive hours driving before he must take an eight-hour rest period. This employer on many occasions would work their drivers 15 to 20 hours before a rest break. One of the drivers actually fell asleep at a red light because he had worked too many hours without sleep.*

2. *The vehicles were not kept up to safety standards. The vehicles had bare tires, light beams out of alignment, cracks in the windshields, brakes slipping or squeaking, air pressure in the tires not correct and on many occasions the vehicles were not clean and/or they stunk.*

3. *The trip ticket that has the information the driver needs to complete the run on many occasions had wrong dates, times, addresses, and telephone numbers.*

4. *The new drivers got almost no training at all.*

5. *The gas re-filling location was not properly maintained creating a fire hazard.*

6. *Company carried no Worker's Compensation Insurance incase a driver got hurt. I was in a wreck and management did not even call me to see how I was doing.*

7. *The facilities had no security at all and were left unlocked. This meant that they could not keep women drivers or dispatchers because the place was not safe.*

8. *The attitude of management and some of the dispatchers toward drivers was not respectful.*

9. *There was no structure for experienced drivers to get an hourly increase to their pay.*

10. *The driver's' facilities were not taken care of; facility usually dirty, trash cans not empty, no soap, paper towel, toilet paper and no office supplies to do paper work.*

11. *Although the drivers had to come to work in a black suite, tie, and white shirt, the cost of buying, cleaning and maintaining the clothing was at the driver's expense.*

12. *The employer provided no employee benefits at all.*

13. *The company required the drivers to do outdated paperwork rather than provide a mobile application.*

14. *The company did not pay more for the early morning runs nor the late night runs.*

15. *The drivers were not provided business cards even though the client needed to stay in touch with the driver.*

16. *Although we advertised that we would provide a newspaper and water, seldom were these items provided*

WHAT BOTHERED me most were the unsafe conditions of the vehicles. The drivers were responsible for filling out repair slips for what needed to be done but once filled out the actual repairs were not done. The only recourse the drivers had was to tell the dispatcher we would not drive that vehicle unless it was brought up to safety standards.

We all can remember the headlines of October 7, 2018 about 20 people being killed in a Limousine in New York's Deadliest U.S. Accident in 9 Years.

STRETCH LIMOUSINES ARE NOT subject to the same safety regulations as passenger cars.

In an article written for Fox News April 10, 2019, State Police said the 2001 Ford Excursion Limo should not have been on the road due to safety issues.

One of the crash victims texted that the limo was in terrible condition before the crash. One wonders when that vehicle was last inspected by the city. As a driver, I was stopped many times by city employees, checking to see if I had a chauffeurs license. One day I was stopped twice. In other words, as a driver, I was inspected a lot. In six years of driving limousines or charter vehicles I have never seen a city employee do one surprise inspection on the vehicle I was driving.

In a USA Today article written January 15, 2019 Governor Cuomo said this: "We are advancing reforms that will give aggressive new powers that will allow authorities to take dangerous vehicles off the roads without delay, hold unscrupulous businesses accountable and increase public safety in every corner of New York," another cover-your-ass statement by the government. I can almost guarantee you that there were laws on the books to take that limousine off the road but government employees did not do their job.

I went to the office that licensed chauffeurs and put stickers on the vehicles, to let the city employees know, that the vehicles I was driving were in an unsafe condition but was told they did not handle complaints. I reminded them that these were the city's rules the company was breaking, why did they not handle complaints?

I decided that I would write the owner of this company that I worked for and list the many problems that I saw with the operation of his company.

———

JUNE 4, 2017

XXXXXXXXXXXX, President
    XXXXXXXXXXXX
    XXXXXXXXXXXX
    Austin, TX XXXXX

SIR:

I WANT to thank you in advance for the invitation to visit with you concerning a number of issues I have, as one of your drivers, with the operations of your limousine services. I thought it would only be fair to give you, in writing, what my concerns are, so that we both can be prepared to discuss them.

SAFETY ISSUES

1) CODE 13-2-55 – A driver who operates a ground transportation service vehicle for 12 consecutive hours must take an eight-hour rest period before resuming operation of a ground transportation service vehicle.

On many occasions this rule is broken to the tune of drivers driving up to 20+ continuous hours without a rest. I have on numerous occasions had to drive 15+ hours without a rest. I have complained about this to a dispatcher and got verbally abused and my schedule for the next week played with. This practice if continued will eventually get a driver and/or a passenger hurt or killed. I can almost guarantee you that in any legal action against your company the plaintiff's lawyer is going to want to see your driving hours record.

2) CODE 13-2-141 – A person may not place a vehicle in service that does not comply with the inspection requirement of this chapter. Code 13-2-142 – The vehicle must be in condition to provide dependable and safe mechanical

operations. Repairs on your vehicles are not done in a timely manner, if at all. I have driven autos with bare tires, light beams out of alignment (which made it hard to see at night), air pressure in the tires incorrect; Hugh cracks in the windshields, brakes slipping or squeaking. I have submitted repair requests on the same problem over and over again without the problem being fixed.

3) Code 13-2-204 – A trip ticket must include the following information. (1) Date of the trip, the name, address, and phone number of the person who booked or paid for the limousine trip. (2) The name, address, and phone number of at least one passenger transported by the limousine on the trip.

On many occasions the ticket does not give me the correct name of the client nor their telephone number. In other words I do not know whom I am picking up or how to get in touch with them. This does not allow me to do my job properly but it also causes me concern about my safety.

4) Code 13-2-405 – A franchise holder who operates a modified ground transportation service vehicle shall provide training for its modified vehicle drivers, its dispatchers, and telephone agents.

I was an experienced driver when hired but had never worked with a dispatcher. I received no training or information on how the dispatcher and I were to interact. I have seen this company hire new drivers who have no experience and give them no or little training. I can't tell you how many times I found one of our new drivers wandering around in the airport with no idea what they are supposed to do.

5) Security of driver facilities (dispatch room, computer room, lounge area and restroom facilities).

The driver facilities have no security at all. The lock on the door has been busted for the almost two years I have worked for this company. I know that this alone caused two women dispatchers concern for their safety. They both are no longer with the company. Strange people often are coming and going through the area and no one knows who they are. Things come up missing and the drivers are blamed. The computers are played with by all the mechanics working next door and often this causes them to crash or our programs to crash.

6) Gas area is a fire hazard.

You want the drivers to fill up their autos when they are finished for the day. I see gas leaks and pump hose cracks.

Driver Care

1. Many times there is no soap, paper towels or toilet paper.
2. Trashcans not emptied in a timely manner.
3. Drivers facility usually dirty
4. No office supplies (scotch tape, stapler, writing/copy paper).
5. Very seldom is there coffee.
6. Dispatcher program out dated.
7. Too much paper work (why are we not using a mobile phone application like "Drive Anywhere").
8. Attitude towards drivers by some managers and some dispatchers is not good.
9. Pay System—there is no increased hourly wage for experience and seniority. I guess your drivers are doomed to be paid minimum wage forever.
10. Does your company have **Workers Compensation Insurance** in case a driver gets hurt on the job? I asked once and was told no.
11. Your company has no employee benefit programs like – Life Insurance, Short-term disability insurance Health Insurance and Retirement Plan.
12. Your company does not have a high enough hourly pay to attract and keep dispatchers.
13. Your company provides us nothing but a cheap tie. The costs of cleaning and upkeep of shirts and suits is our expense.
14. Early morning runs (3 am to 6 am) should pay more.
15. Out of town runs should pay more.

Customer Care

1. The inside of our cars are not properly cleaned and some of them stink.
2. The umbrellas that you buy are cheap and break usually on the first use.
3. You will not furnish business cards so that we can give our client our phone number when we are separated.
4. Although each ticket requires us to provide water and a newspaper to our clients most of the time there is no water or it is locked up in the dispatcher area where we can't get at it. I have never seen any newspapers provided for our clients.

Mr. XXXXXXXXX, I have been in the business world a long time. I have a Master's Degree in Financial Services and have consulted with small business for 42 years. I have been a senior Vice President of a Fortune 500 company. This I can tell you with certainty; **Take *care of your employees and they will take care of you.*** Unfortunately I do not get the feeling, I as one of your drivers, that I am being taken care of. I see a lot of your money being spent to take care of the needs of the people who lease your properties but very little spent taking care of the needs of your drivers.

I REALIZE that by attaching this to an email to all your employees will cause me problems, but I do want the many friends I have made here to know that you have been made aware of some of your drivers concerns. Yes Mr. XXXXXXXXXXX, I do want to continue driving for you. I look forward to our meeting.

SINCERELY,

———————

THE COMPANY MADE some progress on addressing some of my complaints but not all. The owner and I got crosswise because of the letter.

I would have to drive forty-five miles to work and forty-five miles back home. I was forced to use the toll road because I could never depend on getting to work on time or home on time because of the traffic congestions and problems with IH 35 highway. The owner and I talked on several occasions about his letting me keep a car in Georgetown, but that never happened. I would use four gallons of gas (at $2.50 per gallon) going and returning from work plus $12.00 worth of tolls. In other words it would cost me $22.00 to go to work each day and get home afterwards. After three years working for this company I gave them my two weeks notice and quit.

I then went to work for another charter company operating out of Georgetown, Texas. This did away with the long commute because their cars were in Georgetown. I drove for this company for about two years and just recently quit because although closer to my home and a nicer atmosphere to work in, I found that some of the driver abuses I have listed permeates all the companies I worked for.

7

TAXI DRIVERS

An article by Michael Goldstein, "Dislocation And Its Discontents: Ride-Sharing's Impact On The Taxi Industry" *states the following:*

"Last year, more people used Uber than yellow cab in New York City, according to the Taxi & Limousine Commission (TLC). Nationally, receipts from Certify software show that in Q1 2014, ride-hailing was a mere 8% of total business traveler ground transportation market, while rental cars were 55% and taxi 37%. By Q1 2018, ride-hailing had grabbed 70.5% of the market, with rental cars getting 23.5& and taxis just 6%.

ONE WONDERS if the playing fields are level. We know that commercial drivers are regulated much more and they have to pay many more fees than ride-hailing drivers. Taxi medallions are required to operate cabs in New York and they were very valuable. Since ride-hailing services began the value of these medallions has dropped as much as 80%. Can you imagine taking out a loan for one million dollars in order to buy one of these medallions and finding out today that it is only worth $200,000 and you have to pay the loan back with a much decreased income stream? Is it any wonder that New York cab owners are killing themselves?

8

BUS DRIVERS

I Goggled Greyhound Bus to get information and found out Laidlaw International, the company that runs **Greyhound** buses that are a fixture of North America's highways, agreed to be **acquired** by First Group of the United Kingdom for $2.8 billion plus debt. Who is First Group, PLC and what do they do:

The largest provider of home-to-school student transportation in North America with a fleet of 42,500 yellow school buses – twice the size of the next largest competitor.

One of the largest providers of outsourced transit management and contracting services in North America.

The only nationwide operator of scheduled intercity coaches, with a unique network of 2,400 destinations across North America and an iconic brand.

One of the largest bus companies in the UK, with 1.6m

passengers per day, serving two thirds of the 15 largest conurbations in the country.

One of the UK's largest and most experienced rail operators, carrying 345m passengers almost nine billion miles last year across our three franchises and our open access operation.

First Group, PLC gross income for North America Operations, which consisted of First Bus (School Buses), First Transit (City Buses) and Grey Hound Bus was 4.684 Billion Dollars. Let's look at the size of these operations:

First Transit – 12,600 Vehicles - 340 Million Passengers
First Student - 42,000 Yellow Busses – 5M Passengers
Greyhound – 1600 vehicles – 4,000 Journey Destinations

The reason the above is important is that First Group, PLC is big enough to sway the pay scale in this industry. The average Greyhound Lines executive compensation is $231,539 a year. The average Greyhound salary for employees ranges from approximately $17,482 per year for Ticket Sales Representative to $65,934 per year for Electronics Technician. The average base salary for a Greyhound Bus Driver is $61,492. According to the FMCSA, for every ten hours **driving**, the **drivers** need to take 8 consecutive hours off. If your company does operate vehicles every day of the week (Like **Greyhound**), your employer may assign you to the 70-hour/8-day schedule.

Here are some complaints Greyhound Bus Drivers had:

- *I absolutely loved my job at Greyhound but I wasn't getting the proper amount of sleep required to drive safely so I resigned my position. Work-Life balance is horrible. The culture is bad and morale is low.*
- *Executive leadership is in it for themselves. Low pay. Basic benefits. Busses are old and outdated and facilities are in poor condition. Employee turnover is high.*
- *If a promising career with a sense of pride and accomplishment is what you're looking for, then STAY AWAY from Greyhound. One of the biggest issues you'll face is being paid or not being paid at all. The buses are dirty and not properly maintained, which results in breakdowns and angry passengers. Instead of fixing the buses properly the first time, Greyhound in its infinite wisdom will reinstall an old corroded coolant hose on a new water pump. Makes sense right? Then when the bus breaks down they'll call a road service tech and another relief bus costing hundreds of dollars or more, which saves the company a bundle. Everything this company does is illogical and nonsensible.*

Is it not amazing that drivers from different driving experiences in the United States, have some of the same complaints?

9

TRUCK DRIVERS

When I was a young boy back in the 50's I always looked up to truck drivers. At that time truck drivers were well paid, well trained and were known as the best drivers on the road. One could always depend on a truck driver stopping to help you if you had an emergency. Truck drivers were respected and other drivers went out of their way to be courteous to them. Also the number of big trucks on the highways compared to cars was not a problem. Let's look at today: truck drivers are not well paid and many of the younger ones are not well trained. Instead of the auto drivers showing respect and courtesy, they might be cursing them. Truck drivers cannot stop to help in an emergency because they are on the clock and are paid by the mile.

What the hell happened?

The Motor Carrier Act of 1980

The government decided they needed to do more regulating of the trucking industry. The law was signed by President Jimmy Carter, who believed the law could make it cheaper to ship things by truck. The drivers opposed this law and the drivers were right. The law did make it easier and cheaper to ship things by truck but the decline in shipping cost came directly out of the driver's pay.

A great article to read for a detail explanation on how this law ruined the pay of truckers is **"Truck driver salaries have fallen by as much as 50% since the 1970s –and experts say a little known law explains why"**, it appeared in The Business Insider, September 26, 2018, and was written by Rachel Premack. The law made it easier for new trucking companies to form. This law was to be about fostering competition and with more competition the cost of shipping would drop. This is what happened, but most of the cost for cheaper shipping by truck came out of the driver's share of the pie. Now we have so many trucks on the road they can't find enough drivers to drive them but still the driver is underpaid. Also there are so many trucks on the highways that automobiles have trouble navigating the truck congestions. Everywhere one looks now days there are signs *Truck Drivers Needed.* Walmart, whose private fleet of 6,500 is one of the largest in the nation is offering a $1,500 bounty for a new trucker.

What is causing this shortage of drivers?

Here is a quote from Orin Zebest "Driver shortage or pay shortage? I'm voting pay shortage. You all know the debate: the media constantly reports that the transportation industry is suffering from a driver shortage; we know the truth. There are plenty of drivers, but exactly how does the transportation industry expect us to make a living on low wages? Particularly with the economy in a meltdown and gasoline and oil prices so ridiculously high? There are plenty of drivers; we just can't afford to drive our trucks". The average truck driver earns $40,000 to $68,000 per year and you'd have to have a lot of experience to get the $68,000. Driving a truck is a tough profession. Your family life lacks, one rarely showers, and one of the major complaints from drivers is that companies treat you like a machine rather than a human. The estimate is that the transportation industry is 125,000 drivers short of what is needed.

Here is the 2018 income of the five largest trucking companies in the US:

- Swift Transportation 5.34 Billion Dollars
- Schneider International 4.98 Billion Dollars
- J. B. Hunt 8.61 Billion Dollars
- LandStar System 4.6 Billion Dollars
- Werner Enterprises 2.5 Billion Dollars

10

THE PROBLEMS WITH SAFETY

*T*he governments, and owners of these charter and limousine companies, all profess to be very interested in safety. It has been my experience that is a bunch of crap. I will restate that in six years working for the industry I never once saw a government surprise inspection on any of the vehicles that I drove, nor the locations that the drivers worked out of.

Safety Problems I Encountered Daily

- *Vehicles not cleaned properly – not only are the outsides not cleaned, the insides are not cleaned. These vehicles need to be cleaned daily with disinfectant. Travelers are sometimes sick and spread germs.*
- *Windshield wipers defective – weather really plays*

havoc with wiper blades causing serious problems with vision when it rains. Also windshield liquid cleaners not being put in the reservoir is a common problem.

- *Blinker lights out*
- *Tire pressures not correct*
- *Headlight alignments not correct*
- *Seat belts not working properly*
- *Motor oil capacity seldom checked*
- *Low Transmission fluid*
- *Worn tires*
- *Wheels not balanced properly*
- *Wheels out of alignment*
- *Breaks not adjusted, worn pads*
- *Driver not sufficiently rested*
- *Drivers not drug tested*
- *While drivers are on the road, dispatchers and owners are texting them and expect a text response, although texting while driving is against the law in many places.*

Drivers can catch a lot of these safety problems but it takes company employees to fix them. I found that most companies do not have personal to spot or fix the above. Companies plan on keeping their vehicles on the road continuously and will just switch drivers; they do not have any type of backup plan if the car breaks down.

The Fox News article "New York limo in deadly 2018 crash had records falsified by Marvis tire shop, district attorney says" goes into detail how work that was supposed to be done on the limo was not done. The company that was paid to do work on the brakes did not complete the work and falsified the records to show work was completed." I have seen this happen in the companies I drove for where the mechanic would say something was fixed but it wasn't, and charged for the work. Drivers can catch a lot of this but who knows how much is not caught?

One would think that these black cars would carry things for their clients like headache pills, indigestion pills, hand cleaner wipes, eye glass wipes, Kleenex, water, umbrellas, breath mints and newspapers. Most vehicles do not carry first aid kits in case someone gets hurt.

I found that if these things are provided the cost of the items usually comes out of the driver's pockets most of time.

11

DRIVER ABUSE

There are so many ways to abuse drivers that I am sure that I will not list them all. I think that this list of driver abuses is so important because a lot of them also affect the safety of the passengers. This list of abuses is as I thought of them and are not prioritized:

- *The number one abuse of Black Car/Charter Drivers is low pay. Most drivers start out at $ 7.25 per hour and no matter the driver experience they may acquire most never get over $ 10.00 per hour.*
- *Scheduling of trips always leans towards maximizing profits.*
- *Scheduling of trips is never about the driver's time behind the wheel, it is always about maximizing the use of the vehicle.*

- *Very seldom is their extra driver compensation for very early or very late trips.*
- *Many companies do not want the drivers to clock in and get paid for the time they use traveling to and from the point of pick up or drop off.*
- *Trips out of town pay the driver the same hourly rate although the company chargers the client more.*
- *Many companies do not build a tip into their rates nor do they ask the client to tip.*
- *Some companies actually steal the tips.*
- *When writing the ticket some companies will allow the rider to use a fictious name and telephone number which hinders the driver from doing his job correctly and makes the driver feel unsafe.*
- *About thirty percent of all tickets I handled had some information that was incorrect, requiring me to track down the incorrect information.*
- *Company letting their gas facilities run out of gas requiring the driver to use his resources to put gas in the vehicle.*
- *Companies not keeping their airport accounts up to date requiring driver to fund entry into holding area out of his pocket.*
- *Companies not paying for tickets received from police officers for out of date safety inspection, light bulbs out, and blinker not working properly.*
- *Companies do not pay for the renewals of the chauffeur licenses.*
- *Companies not providing suits, shirts or ties.*

- *Companies not paying for the cleaning of clothing required by the company.*
- *Not paying overtime on a daily basis.*
- *Scheduling the driver for six or seven days of driving to get forty hours a week.*
- *Scheduling a driver to take a 12:00 PM trip, which would put the driver home a 01:30 AM and then scheduling the driver for a 05:00 AM run the next day.*
- *Requiring drivers to watch phone applications on late plane arrival times and clock in only when the plane gets close to landing time.*

12

AIRPORT/AIRPLANES

I did many runs to private runways or airports and the private plane locations for the most part were very clean and well run. It is amazing to me how for profit businesses who have to compete for business always seem to run much better than anything connected to the government. These private establishments always treated the black car drivers with respect and tried to make us comfortable. They realized that we were very important to the success of their business.

I can only speak about one commercial airport because most of my runs were to and from the airport in Austin, Texas. This airport used to be an Air Force Base and the city of Austin took it over many years ago. They are still working on converting it to a commercial airport. Austin is a city that the world has found. Austin is the capitol of Texas and has the University of Texas with fifty thousand plus students. It is a very big computer and software city and it has grown in the last twenty years to almost a million in population. The city is trying to redo the airport from a sleepy small town airport to a huge city airport.

In my opinion most of the huge amount of construction is happening to maximize profits. They have built increased plane deplaning facilities and increased vehicle parking facilities, but the entrance of the airport is very unsafe. There are two levels to enter the airport and both levels have the same dangerous situations. All the people coming from parking areas, buses, taxies, limousine services and off airport parking facilities have to cross four lanes of traffic. This traffic consists of autos dropping off passengers, charter services picking up and dropping off and Uber and Lyft services. During the busy times at the airport this creates an extremely dangerous situations for pedestrians and vehicles. I am surprised that more people are not injured or killed. The only way to fix the problem is to build a skyway cross-walk for the upper level and a tunnel crosswalk for the lower level. As I see it these are not going to get built unless more people get killed. Again profits take precedence over safety.

All commercial drivers have to pay a fee for a tag to be able to pick up passengers from the airport. Commercial drivers also have to go through a gate and pay $3.50 each time they come to pick someone up. No charge for dropping off. If a driver has to wait, they must wait in the holding area, which is almost never cleaned properly. The bathrooms are almost always nasty.

One of the amazing things is that if you are a limousine

driver you must stop your vehicle, open the trunk and all the doors, so that the vehicle can be inspected. This is supposedly to stop suicide bombers. None of the cabs, charter services and most buses are inspected. I asked one day why only the limousines were inspected. I was told that they are the only ones where the drivers are allowed to get out of our vehicles. Now this is just me, but isn't the definition of a suicide bomber someone who also blows himself up?

The airport just recently built a mobile lot parking area that has a gas station, four places for restaurants and restroom facilities. Nice and clean and shiny for about two months and then the lack of care takes over. Why is it that government run facilities are usually dirty? Of course everything that is for sale in any airport is way overpriced. One becomes a prisoner in their facilities and they overcharge you for anything you buy and you are supposed to like it.

THE INTERNET in this airport is terrible. Everything that we do in our industry is run by phone applications. We get our tickets, our driving instructions and all the information on time schedules via the phone. When the Internet is not working most drivers are hampered or put out of business. Can you imagine what airline passengers go through trying to use their phones?

I can remember when flying by air was a memorable and exciting experience. We used to wear suits and nice dresses. The airline fed you great meals and drinks and if they found out one had a birthday or anniversary they celebrated with you with a free bottle of champagne. The flight attendants were always polite and caring and because they were, one gave them the respect they deserved. The planes for the most part were on time and comfortable and most of the flights were straight through flights. No airline charged you for your bags so there was no need to bring bags into the plane with you.

Now we have what I call the cattle car effect. If you like to people watch, the best place in town is your local airport. It is amazing what people wear or don't wear in an airport or airplane. A lot have not bathed or shaved in days and they smell like it. Some airlines do not have assigned seats so not only do you have to wait to board, you have to scuffle for a seat. It seems like one in three people have to have some kind of animal with them. There is no such thing as hot meals; you are lucky if you get a bag of peanuts. All the seats are made for someone that is three foot tall with no knees. Straight through flights are almost a thing of the past and getting anywhere on time is a blessing. Is it any wonder that passengers are rude to flight attendants? I know when I pick up someone who just got off a plane; chances are that they will need a few minutes to come back to the real world.

Airports do all they can to make sure that people can come to and leave their airport. They really do not care if the providers of the transportation make a living and survive or not. If fact in a lot of cases the airport will charge the provider a fee for the privilege of providing transportation to their customers. There are many providers of transportation for the airport in Austin, Texas. Fares range from free to $15.00 to go downtown, which is about ten miles away.

I want to say a few words in this section about Uber and Lyft (much more said in other sections) that pertains to airports and airport congestion. An article written by Ben Lovejoy July 27, 2018 titled "Ride-sharing services like Uber and Lyft making car congestion worse, not better, study" (6) suggests that Uber and Lyft vehicles do not minimize congestion but increase congestion. I believe this, having worked in and around airports for the past several years. Not only are there more vehicles but these ride sharing drivers clog the traffic by taking up two lanes to drop passengers off.

An article in Smart Cities, May 19, 2018 titled *Uber and Lyft are the biggest contributors to San Francisco's growing traffic problem*" (8) states "Traffic congestion in San Francisco went up by about 60% from 2010 to 2016, and Uber and Lyft were responsible for more than half that increase, according to a new study in Science Advances.

13

ROADS AND HIGHWAYS

First of all I have to tell you that I think there is a committee of twelve people in Austin, Texas, who watch screens that have all the road cameras going to them. As soon as this committee sees any part of the road or highway working properly without any problems they send some kind of construction crew out to that road and they start blocking the road off and causing traffic jams. Most of the time the things they use to block traffic, are there way before the construction starts and way after construction ends. What is scary is the big trucks they park to protect the workers, they will certainly kill the driving public but the worker will be protected.

Have you ever noticed that one never sees a policeman, when there is a traffic jam, trying to direct traffic but we always see them when traffic is flowing nicely, policemen giving speeding tickets?

Why does construction work have to be done during the daytime when traffic is busiest? Why can't we do the work on the roads at night when there is little traffic? If you make that request to the government powers that be, they will tell you that we must be concerned for the safety of the workers. What about the safety of the drivers that are stuck in these construction traffic jams?

Why does the Texas government allow eighteen-wheelers to drive 75 and 85 miles per hour on our highways? These trucks are over sixty feet long, weigh many tons driving on hot pavement with temperatures in excess of 140 degrees in the summer time. They are blowing tires right and left and they are clogging the traffic flow. We used to have laws that restricted the trucks from driving over sixty-five miles per hour so the auto traffic could pass them. Now the automobiles are dodging rubber from their blown out tires and one can imagine how fast a car must go to pass a truck doing 85 mph. There is a law that these eighteen-wheelers are not to be in the left lane, but the police are not enforcing the law. What the automobile driver ends up with, is trucks in all lanes of the highway and no way to get around them.

Around the city of Austin a driver can go almost nowhere without going on a toll road and paying a toll. If the city adds another lane to an existing road, chances are they will make it a toll lane. In my opinion the citizens in most cases have already paid for the road and have kept it repaired for years through the gas taxes they pay; why should they now have to pay a toll to drive on it?

Austin, Texas is one of the busiest cities in the nation and they are growing so fast they can't keep up with the growth. The city will continue to let developers build skyscrapers, malls, apartments and housing developments knowing full well they do not have the infrastructure to sustain all this growth. So we have a city that takes you an ungodly amount of time to drive into and get out of. Once one gets into Austin the city has every possible parking space metered so they can collect more blood money from you. Still no one can find a place to park.

If you want to march to show your displeasure with anything that is happening in the world, then Austin, Texas is the city to do it in. Almost every day there are marchers with bullhorns, clogging the traffic flow, to hell with the drivers, they can wait.

Another thing that tends to piss me off as a professional automobile driver in the city of Austin, Texas is all the special lanes and rules for other forms of transportation. Let me just name a few:

- *Horse Drawn Buggies*
- *Golf Cart Type Vehicles*
- *Bicycles*
- *Buses*
- *Bicycle Drawn Buggies*
- *Battery Driven Bicycles*
- *Battery Driven Scooters*

The city busses have their own lanes on a lot of the streets. Now that must be nice for the bus drivers. The rest of us have to fight for our driving space. Now the government will tell you that it is because these busses are so big that they need special room to maneuver. I challenge any reader: the next time you pass a city bus in Austin, count the riders. Count over a period of time and one will see a bus that takes up a huge amount space on the road averages about 4 to six riders.

Have you ever noticed that although bicycle riders are supposed to go by the same road rules we are, they seldom do? Austin, like a lot of cities, is providing special lanes for bicycles. They say this is good because it will cut down on auto traffic. Now we have fewer lanes for automobiles and people riding bicycles not going by the rules of the road. This makes all us much safer?

If you want to make driving in a city even scarier, bring in little green battery powered scooters. Now we have mobile people all over the road and sidewalks, not only are they running people off the sidewalks into the roads but they are now in the roads also. I have even seen two big people on one scooter.

I am not an engineer (thank God) but even I know that red lights need to be synchronized. Drive almost any roads in any city in this country and you will find red lights that are not synchronized and the traffic stacking up because of it. Just think of all the time wasted for drivers, the wear and tear on vehicles, the gas wasted and the pollution in the air because red lights that are not synchronized. I will bet money that if there were a button on your dash that you could punch to pay the city for synchronization of red lights that this problem would be corrected immediately. I probably should not have said that, next thing you know there will be a spot on your utility bill charging for the synchronization of red lights.

It is my opinion that the engineers who design our roadways and the bureaucrats who make the laws, have to take some of the responsibility for the carnage on our roadways and lawlessness of our drivers.

Now let's give a shout out to the drivers on the road. Drivers that are not required to take Continuing Education Courses (CEs), drivers who are not required to test their driving skills on a regular basis, and drivers who are preoccupied with telephones, radios and occupants.

The state requires that the vehicle pass auto inspection every year but lets the drivers go without testing.

14

DRIVERS ON THE ROADS

O h my God what a subject to tackle. First let's start out with the licensing of drivers. Once licensed (if you are not a commercial driver), in Texas, you may never be tested again except for your eyesight. Now consider these facts, in almost all professions one has to take continuing education courses and periodically be tested for different phases of the industry you are in. I know that when I was in the Financial Services Industry I had to take thirty-six continuing education hours every year to make sure I stayed proficient. I have been driving for sixty years and I have never been re-tested for my driver's license. I have had to take tests for my commercial driver's license but never for my individual license.

Can you imagine how many people are on our roads that have been driving for years and have never upgraded their driving skills?

All these people on the roads with diminished driving skills and knowledge and the state does not even know who they are and I wonder if they care.

I firmly believe that individuals should be tested with a written and a driving test in order to renew their driver's licenses once every five years. A defensive driver course should be mandatory every ten years. I can hear all the moans out there now. Look people, when you drive you not only have the lives of the people in your vehicle in your hands but the lives of people in other vehicles.

Let's talk about the physical tests drivers must go through. An eye test that anyone who has vision problems has a good chance of passing. There is no hearing test at all. Anyone who is hard of hearing can drive. What does that mean? It means that we have people driving who cannot hear your horn warning them of danger or problems. If you wear glasses for corrected vision, one has a notice on your license, saying that you must be wearing your glasses when you drive. Why do we not have a hearing test for prospective drivers and if their hearing is bad require them to wear hearing aids? I am amazed how many of the drivers on the road can't hear, especially in our older population.

LET'S get down to the driving habits of the general public. In my six years of commercial driving there were at least two times a day that some driver tried to kill me. Below are some of the common mistakes that drivers make:

1. ***Riding the bumper.*** *I am amazed how many people do not realize that if I have to slam on my brakes, you, your car and everyone in it has a problem.*
2. ***Short stopping distance.*** I am trying to leave enough room in between me and the next car so that I will have enough space to stop should that car slam on its brakes. Please do not cut into my braking space.
3. ***Use the blinkers.*** It just takes a twitch of the finger to let me and everyone else know what you are going to do. We do not read minds.
4. ***Dim your lights.*** If you do not need high beams please do not have them on. If you need them please dim them when approaching cars.
5. ***The left lane is always the passing or turning lane.*** Please stay out of it if you're not turning or passing.
6. ***Watch the speed limit.*** Going too fast or too slow is dangerous to other drivers.
7. ***Leave fifteen minutes early.*** It is amazing how many drivers are late to something and put other drivers in danger going too fast.
8. ***Do not multitask.*** All one's attention should be on the task of driving—not on any other project.

9. *No phone/texting.* Never text while driving and do not use the telephone unless you have a Bluetooth.

10. *No loud radio.* Remember an important part of driving is being able to hear danger coming.

11. *When merging be diligent.* It is your responsibility to see oncoming traffic and to merge into traffic. This will probably mean you will have to slow down or speed up but you must look and make that decision.

12. *Slow down on access roads.* It is a good idea to slow down on access roads so that one will have better reaction time when people get off the highway and when people on side roads are trying to access the highway.

13. *When merging yield to larger vehicles.* I know most people believe when they merge they have the right of way. I drive a forty-foot Class "A" motor home and a tow car that is fifteen feet long. The RV, with the towing rig, is almost seventy feet long. The total rig weighs about ten tons. I need a good football field to stop. An eighteen-wheeler, which is longer and weighs a lot more, needs two football fields to stop. **When you are dead it doesn't matter who had the right of way.**

14. *Red lights.* Yellow light means you should be stopping not speeding up. At green light always make sure you are safe before you proceed.

15. ***When it's raining or snowing slow down.*** Slick streets can kill you.

16. ***Truckers.*** a. You know as well as I do, that no tire is made that will handle 30 tons doing 80 miles an hour on payment that is 140 degrees. b. Please do not try and pass another truck if it is doing the max speed limit, you're not going to pass it and you will have a lot of irritated auto drivers stacked up behind you. c. Please leave enough room in between trucks so that autos may pass. d. Dump trucks, the law requires you to have a cover over your load. Please make sure it is in good repair and you are using it. I am tired of paying for nicked or broken windshields. And please take those stupid signs off that tell me to stay behind you 200 feet and that you are not responsible for damaged windshields. There is no way I can stay behind you by 200 feet if I am driving on Texas highways. You are responsible for the rocks you through into windshields no matter what stupid sign you put on your truck.

15

CUSTOMERS

Having driven charter vehicles and black cars for six years I can honestly tell you that 95% of my customers have been great. Politeness and courtesy were the rule. Most of them want to have some type of conversation with the driver.

I am now going to discuss the other 5%. Not so much to bitch but more to educate:

- *When you get into a vehicle for hire, do not ever think that the driver is some dummy. You will be pleasantly surprised to find some very intelligent drivers who can have a discussion with you on almost any subject.*
- *The driver does not need or want driving instructions nor directions from you (unless they ask).*
- *Don't assume the driver knows all the greatest places to eat or drink in the city.*

- *The bigger the city the more the driver will rely on a GPS.*
- *Just as you, the rider, will have bad days, so will the driver.*
- *Always keep in mind that the driver makes most of his/her income from tips. Any tip is appreciated but be realistic, if you will tip a waitress 20% for delivering your food then a driver who is responsible for the safety of your life is also worth a 20% tip. The only way one can be assured that your driver will receive your tip is for you to give it to the driver yourself. Yes, I hate to say this but the people who own the companies, will sometimes steal the driver's tip and then tell the driver you did not tip.*
- *Always keep your cell phone charged and on; this is how the driver is going to find you.*
- *Bags should never weigh more than 50 pounds. Please remember that in your travels someone is going to have to lug that bag in and out of cars; also remember they have been lifting bags all day long.*
- *Kindness is always appreciated. The driver cannot control everything that happens.*
- *If you have a cold or the flu please cover your mouth and nose when sneezing or coughing.*
- *Please take your garbage with you.*

THERE IS NEVER **an excuse for rudeness**

16

MECHANICAL REPAIRS

Yes I am in my 70's and can remember eating a hamburger that cost 25 cents. My first pickup truck cost $1500.00 brand new. Yes I have my faculties still and I know there is such a thing as inflation.

Give me a frigging break. No new pickup truck or automobile is worth $80,000.00+. If they were made to last 20 years, made so the owner could fix 80% of what needed to get fixed and gave us 80 miles to the gallon, maybe. They are made so that the average person who has any mechanical skills can't work on them, if one gets 10 years service one is lucky and miles per gallon ranges from 12 to 20. Half the time, one cannot even get to the battery to put water into it or change the oil.

Have you noticed that if you take your vehicle in to almost any repair shop, be they a dealer or an independent, the bill will most likely be over a thousand dollars no matter what you are having repaired? The repair shops all go by this book of prices for repairs that inflates the time needed to make the repair. I can't prove it (because customers never get to see this book) but I think the time inflation is one hundred percent at least. In other words if the actual time to make the repair is one hour the book shows two hours.

Most shops charge $125.00 plus per hour labor. Have you ever had a shop tell you when you went to get your vehicle it did not take all the time they charged you for and they were reducing their total charge? Most men can relate to this story: Twenty years ago one could buy spark plugs for $5.00 each and put them in yourself. For a four-cylinder motor one could put points and plugs in for $30.00. Nowadays the auto maker has made it so hard to get to these plugs that the repair shop can charge you $500.00 to replace four spark plugs.

The shop will not let you bring any parts in for them to install. The parts must be bought through the shop where you are getting the work done. This is so the shop can put their charge on the part to increase their profit.

I can remember taking my RV in because the step to get in it would not come out. I had already deduced that it was not the motor but a relay that went out. The relay cost about $70.00 and could be ordered on line. The RV dealer told me that the whole mechanism that included the motor had to be replaced because you could not get individual pieces to the mechanism. I gave him the web site and information on the part and they still would only replace the whole mechanism. The whole mechanism cost $390.00. Now let's play a little mind game. If their markup was only 10% they made $39.00 extra. Imagine a dealership using three million dollars a year in parts.

Think back and remember how many times you have caught dishonest mechanics. I have caught a mechanic telling me I had an oil leak that would cost a $1000.00 worth of work to fix and on inspection find that they had sprayed oil on the under carriage so it would appear like there was a leak. I have caught a mechanic cutting wires so that he could make repairs to the electrical system. I have had a mechanic trying to charge my daughter for automatic transmission fluid flushing at 30,000 miles when the time to flush is 100,000 miles.

The cost of mechanical repairs of vehicles used by commercial drivers has increased to the point that they are ridiculous. I can guarantee you that this increase is not coming out of the pocket of the owner, executives or stockholders of the company. The owners, before they raise their prices, will take cost increases out of the drivers' pay.

17

COMPANIES GET RICHER WITH SELF-DRIVING VEHICLES

The transportation corporations have squeezed as much profit as they can get cutting wages and benefits and the drivers are starting to raise hell so they are throwing billions of dollars at producing self-driving vehicles. Most companies will tell you that their biggest expense on their profit and loss statement is the cost of labor so if they can do away with that cost the company could double, triple or quadruple their profits, **yay, more money for shareholders and executives.**

An article in the Los Angeles Times by Steven Greenhouse, September 22, 2016, estimates that driverless cars will cost the country five million jobs (3% of the work force). Most of these workers are not college graduates and a lot do not have high school diplomas. It is not just the drivers who will lose their jobs but a lot of other people who work in the transportation industry. How are these families going to eat and pay for housing?

From what I read driverless vehicles are about two to three years away. I have heard nothing from the government on any programs that will help these people get through the transition period and to be re-trained. You damn well know that the companies who lay them off are not going to pay to retrain them. So once again the people who do the work to make corporations big and rich are getting screwed.

18

GOVERNMENT

I worked in the financial services arena for forty-two years in investments and insurance. I did business through a broker dealer and I was also a registered investment advisor. For forty-two years I had a government official do surprise audits on me at least once a year, and some years there were two or three audits. One morning you would go to your office and there would be one or two auditors waiting for you, to do a surprise audit. If you did not want to be audited, then you lost your license and could not work in that profession. These surprise audits really kept people on their toes. One worked to always be ready for an audit.

Just think if companies repairing autos, RV's and buses had someone bring a vehicle in and the government checked the establishment for correct repairs and pricing? What if this secret auditor brought in a vehicle that was in perfect condition and the shop charged him for repairs his vehicle did not need and the government caught them. What if an auditor was sent into a dealership and audited the hours they charged for repairs verses the hours they actually use for the repairs, caught discrepancies in favor of the vehicle owner? What if when a repair shop was caught cheating their customers, the business was shut down until corrective action was completed? It would not be long before the word would spread throughout the city and all repair shops would always be ready for an audit.

Now let's look at what surprise audits would accomplish in the driving industry. First, the auditor would verify that business was making sure that all their vehicles were in top mechanical shape by inspecting the vehicles. The auditor, by checking payroll (hours worked in a day) would find out if the business abused their drivers by working them too many hours without sleep. The auditor, by checking payroll records would find out if the employer was cheating their drivers out of pay. What if an auditor actually rode with a driver and could asses if the driver was trained properly and knew what he was doing?

While I was a driver, the vehicles I drove got inspected once a year when the permit was renewed. You know that the business was going to send that vehicle to be inspected in excellent condition. What about the other 100,000 miles that vehicle was to be driven? Remember the limousine in New York that crashed and kill so many people; *an inspection would have taken that vehicle off the road.*

FINAL THOUGHTS

Six years driving professionally has given me a new perspective on drivers, professional drivers, and the government entities that regulate driving and build our roads. I do know now that our training, testing and licensing of the driver needs a closer look. We have way too many drivers who do not know the rules of the road. A license to drive should require that every driver have continuing education credits throughout their driving life so that they can keep up with the changes in vehicles, driving conditions and laws. Every driver should be required to take an intensive defensive driving course every five years, then pass a written test and an actual driving test in order to renew their license.

We also have way too many drivers on the roads that have hearing and sight problems. Presently almost anyone can pass the vision test and there is no hearing test at all. Not being able to read road signs nor hear someone honking causes problems.

After driving in major cities in Texas (Houston, Dallas, Ft. Worth, Austin and San Antonio) I have some simple advice for them. Quit worrying about how big the city can get and how much money in taxes/fees you can bring in and worry more about the quality of life and safe driving in your city. Some of the simple things that can be done that can make the driving experience better are:

1. synchronize your lights

2. make repairs to the roads at night

3. high-rise buildings must provide parking

4. quit nickel and diming people for parking

5. paint your strips so people can see them

6. demonstrations during certain hours only

7. do a study to find dangerous road situations

8. start worrying about light pollution at night

9. aggressive policing of pedestrians

10. limit vehicles in downtown area

There are too many accidents, injuries and deaths on our highways, I believe this problem starts with the design. Too much emphasis on moving automobiles and too little emphasis on the safety of driving. Not enough future planning for our highways. It seems that we are always trying to fix a problem rather than being pro-active. A good example is the engineers know that traffic is going to out grow a section of the highway in five years. Why not build the highway or make upgrades so that even with growth it will last ten or fifteen years? Why not build our highways first, plan and limit the growth around them? Our highways have speed limits on 75, 80 and 85 miles per hour. Our highways, tires and reaction time cannot handle these speeds. We all know that if the speed limit is 85 miles per hour then the average driver will go 90 miles per hour.

Trucking is the lifeblood of our nation and we need to hit a happy medium between trucks and automobiles on our highways. I believe trucking maximum speed limit should be five miles lower than automobiles. This one change would make all the difference in safe driving and highway congestion. This use to be the law in Texas, but the big trucking companies squawked and got the law changed. Another example of money verses safety in our highway and road systems.

"From a man who remembers towns with dirt roads and having only one traffic light on Main Street, to a professional driver who has worked in the honorable profession of driving people from all walks of life, I encourage future drivers—with their totally automatic cars and even their flying cars one day—to be courteous and share the road."

Sammy Lee Gott

ALSO BY SAMMY LEE GOTT

"When Love Doesn't Start At Home: Surviving a Dysfunctional Family"

It was hard being one of four boys growing up in the 1940s in a dysfunctional family. Throw in alcoholic parents, a hot tempered pure-bred American Indian mother, a father running secret missions for the military, and three wild brothers and you got a mix of family craziness.

This is a beautiful and engaging book about surviving and prospering after growing up in a dysfunctional family. It is told by a man who is a brother, husband, father, veteran, and overall good guy who has a lot of life lessons to share with the world.

For more information, visit http://www. sammyleegott.com/WLDSAH-info

---

"Life is a Series of Jokes"

This is a story of all the things that happen to a man from pre-birth to age 75 This book covers the events that a man has no control over but which affects his life and what direction his life goes. These twists and turns in life are very humorous and are accentuated by hundreds of jokes that fit the situations.

Sammy Lee Gott has been a son, brother, husband, father, soldier, and all around good guy for the last 75 years. During his life's journey, he has learned the power of humor. This is a collection of his personal story and plenty of jokes he's discovered.

For more information, visit http://sammyleegott.com/LIASOJ-info

---

"Neither Man Nor Woman is Spelled S.A.I.N.T."

We are in the crossroad of hate and love between men and women in the United States and right now hate is winning. This book explores some of the ways that we as a nation can be more on the side of love first by defining what love is and suggestions on how men and women can make a difference in this battle.

For more information, visit http://sammyleegott.com/NMNWISS-info

www.ingramcontent.com/pod-product-compliance
Lightning Source LLC
Chambersburg PA
CBHW021136020426
42331CB00005B/796

* 9 7 8 1 9 4 8 9 9 7 4 3 0 *